SING through the DAY

SING

the plough publishing house

Rifton, New York   1969

through the DAY

NINETY SONGS FOR YOUNGER CHILDREN

Compiled and Edited by the SOCIETY OF BROTHERS

Musical Arrangments by Marlys Swinger
Illustrations by Jeanie, Joanie and Judy
Music and Words hand-lettered by Gillian Barth

SING THROUGH THE DAY

First Printing, October 1, 1968, 1400 copies
Second Printing, April 1, 1969, 2500 copies

Printed at the Plough Press, Farmington, Pennsylvania
Library of Congress Catalog Card Number 68-9673
Standard Book Number 87486-005-9

Acknowledgments

The Society of Brothers is grateful for the permission granted in the use of the material which follows. Every effort has been made to locate all sources, and in some cases these could not be found. Any corrections necessary will be made in future editions of this book.

Special thanks are due to the British Broadcasting Corporation, the British Museum, Evans Brothers Limited, Jonathan Cape Limited, the Music Publishers' Association Limited, and the National Christian Education Council for their efforts in helping us locate sources of certain English songs; also to Dr. Percy M. Young for his kind assistance.

"Birthday Presents" from *The Whole World Singing,* compiled by Edith Lovell Thomas; reprinted by permission of the Friendship Press, New York. Copyright 1950.

"Boats Sail on the Rivers" from *Sing-Song* by Christina Rosetti. Reprinted with permission of the Macmillan Company. Copyright 1924 by the Macmillan Company.

"Bumblebees Are Humming," "Dance, Little Maiden," "Dearest Sun" ("Sun Song"), and "Pit, Pat, Pat" ("Home in the Rain"), from *Children's Sing-Song from Sweden,* by Alice Tegner, translated into English by Maisie Radford, published by Augener, London. By permission of Galaxy Music Corp., New York, for Galliard, Ltd., London.

"Corn in the Wind" by Rodney Bennett and Joan Bennett from *Child Education;* reprinted by permission of Joan Bennett.

"Daisies" by Frank Dempster Sherman, reprinted and set to music by permission of the Houghton Mifflin Company.

"Easter Greeting" by Laura E. Richards, reprinted by permission of Allenson and Company, London.

"The Fairy Flute" and "Singing Time" by Rose Fyleman, reprinted and set to music by permission of the Society of Authors as literary representative of the Estate of the late Rose Fyleman.

"Firefly" from *Under the Tree* by Elizabeth Madox Roberts. Copyright 1922 by B. W. Huebsch, Inc., 1950 by Ivor S. Roberts. Reprinted by permission of the Viking Press, Inc. The combination of words and music is by Edith Lovell Thomas from *The Whole World Singing,* Friendship Press.

"For the Golden Corn" by E. Gould and E. Smith, and "O Dandelion, Yellow as Gold" by Noreen Bath, from *Child Education;* reprinted by permission of Evans Brothers Limited.

"Go to Bethlehem," "Heaven's Gate Has Opened," and "Up, Little Hans," reprinted by permission of the Cooperative Recreation Service, Inc., Delaware, Ohio.

"Go to Sleep" from *Folk Jingles of American Children* by Dorothy G. M. Howard (Doctoral Dissertation, School of Education, New York University, 1938). Used by permission of Dr. Howard.

"God Made the Shy, the Wild Ones" ("Elizabeth's Carol") by Elizabeth Gould and Hugh S. Roberton, reprinted by permission of J. Curwen and Sons, Ltd., copyright 1951.

"Good Evening, Shining Silver Moon" ("The Moon"), "The Magic Pony," and "The Obedient Kitten" from *A Child's Book of Songs,* copyright 1928; used by permission of the American Book Company.

"The House of the Mouse" from *Another Here and Now Story Book* by Lucy Sprague Mitchell. Copyright 1937 by E. P. Dutton & Co., Inc. Renewal copyright 1965 by Lucy Sprague Mitchell. Reprinted and set to music by permission of the publishers.

"I Am Quite Big" ("Playmates") from *Sixty Songs for Little Children* and "Squirrel Nutkin" from *Second Sixty Songs for Little Children,* reprinted by permission of the Oxford University Press.

"I Held a Lamb" by Kim Worthington, reprinted and set to music by permission of *Child Life,* copyright 1954.

"I'm Little White Clover" ("Song of the White Clover Fairy") from *Flower Fairies of the Summer* by Cicely M. Barker and Olive Linnell. Reprinted by permission of the publisher, Blackie and Son, Ltd.

"Indian Harvest" from *Rhythms and Rimes* of *The World of Music* series. Copyright 1936, 1943, by Ginn and Company. Used with permission.

"Indian Lullaby" by Walter H. Aiken. Reprinted by permission of the Willis Music Company.

"Little Donkey Close Your Eyes" (abridged) from *The Fish with*

Acknowledgements

the Deep Sea Smile by Margaret Wise Brown, published by E. P. Dutton and Co., Inc., copyright 1938 and 1956 by Roberta B. Rauch.

"Little Red Bird" used by permission of Stainer and Bell, London, and the Galaxy Music Corporation.

"Mary's Lullaby" by Ivy O. Eastwick. Reprinted and set to music by special permission of the author and *Jack and Jill* Magazine, copyright 1947, The Curtis Publishing Company.

"Mud" by Polly Chase Boyden from *Child Life* Magazine, copyright 1930, 1958 by Rand McNally & Company. Reprinted and set to music by permission of the publisher and Barbara Boyden Jordan, the author's representative.

"Oro, My Little Boat" from the record *So Early in the Morning* collected by Diane Hamilton, Tradition Record: TLP 1034. By permission of the Everest Record Group, Los Angeles.

"Shepherds Come A-Running" from *A Book of Christmas Carols,* selected and illustrated by Haig & Regina Shekerjian. Arranged for Piano by Robert de Cormier. Copyright 1963 by Haig & Regina Shekerjian. Used by permission of Harper & Row, Publishers.

"Song of the Bunnies" from the book *Nibble Nibble* by Margaret Wise Brown, published by Young Scott Books, copyright October 1959; by permission of Jeanne Hale, literary agent for the author.

"The Sun" by John Drinkwater, reprinted and set to music by permission of the Houghton Mifflin Company.

"The Sun Is Rising Out of Bed" ("Morning Song"), words by John Ferguson to an English folk tune, from *Together We Sing,* Follett Publishing Company, copyright 1952. Used with permission.

"This Is the Day" used by permission of the composer, T. Janet Surdam. Copyright 1953.

"Three Kings" from *God's Wonderful World* by Agnes Leckie Mason and Phyllis Brown O'Hanian. Copyright 1954 by Agnes Leckie Mason and Phyllis Brown O'Hanian. Reprinted by permission of Random House, Inc.

"To Bethlehem I would Go" from *Seven Czechoslovak Carols,* published by Schott & Company, Ltd., copyright 1942. Permission granted by Schott & Company, Ltd., and Associated Music Publishers, Inc.

The following songs are published for the first time in English, having been translated from the German by members of the Society of Brothers.

"Dainty Little Butterfly" ("Schmetterling und Blume"), "The Easter Hare" ("Vom Osterhaas"), and "Marie in the Meadow" ("Klein Marie") from *Hundert Kinderlieder* by Edwin Kunz. Reprinted by permission of Orell Füssli Verlag, Zürich.

"The Earth Needs the Raindrops" ("Die Erde braucht Regen") from *Bruder Singer* published by Bärenreiter-Verlag, Kassel and Basel.

"Good Morning, Dear Children" ("Guten Morgen, mein Liebchen") by Walter Rein in *Unser Fröhlicher Gesell.* Reprinted by permission of Möseler Verlag, Wolfenbüttel, who hold all rights. Copyright 1956.

"Sunshine and Rain" ("Sonne und Regen müssen ja sein") by Margarete Derlien. Reprinted by permission of Bärenreiter-Verlag, Kassel and Basel, who hold all rights.

For everyone who has a childlike heart

During his early innocent period the child is still completely at one with the whole creation, so full of trust to all living things that he can talk with animals as if they were people, so full of wonder as he takes in all big things and all little things: stars in the sky, flowers in the field, or a little pebble in the sandpile. There is nothing created that does not captivate the child's interest, and that he does not try to grasp with all his heart.

from a talk given by
Eberhard Arnold *in* 1933.

Introduction

Do you like to sing with children? We do! And because we would like to share the songs we have been singing with our children through the years, we've made a book, including many of our favorites.

This collection of songs comes out of the community life of a group known as the Society of Brothers. In these communities, families and single people live together in a life of full sharing, based on the example of the early Christians. The Society makes its home in three places in the United States: Rifton, New York; Farmington, Pennsylvania; and Norfolk, Connecticut.

In these three communities, the children spend a part of each day with other children of their age group, and share many experiences together. These groups range from younger children through the eighth grade. It is natural for our children to sing together (one of the favorites of the youngest is "Hallelujah" on page 117), and all the everyday times—morning, play-time, mealtimes, going-to-bed—bring tunes and words to their lips.

Parents share closely with their children and the teachers in all that they experience through the daily life in the community. (A fuller picture of the life of our children is given in the book *Children in Community*.)

Some of the songs in this book (for example, "Dwarf Song" and "The Princess Was a Lovely Child") have been sung since the beginning years of our life together, dating back to the early 1920's in Germany. At this time a small number of people, under the guidance of Eberhard Arnold, chose to live together in a life of love and service as a witness to brotherhood. Other individuals and families came to join with the first few in this life of searching together. In time, after much hardship and struggle, a farm was purchased. This community was forced to leave Germany in the late 1930's because of the persecution from the Nazis, and for a time made its home in England. From there, another forced exodus was made to Paraguay, the only country which would immediately accept immigrants during war time. (The story of the beginning years of the community is told in the book, *Torches Together,* by Emmy Arnold.)

Throughout all the years of moving about and of living and discovering together, our lives have been enriched by song. As people of various nationalities and from all walks of life have joined with us, the songs have become increasingly varied. Also, new songs have been written through special occasions or experiences—a song for a new baby, a new birthday song, or one for a festive occasion. The songs in this book are both old and new, but all belong to the experience of the childlike heart. Because we feel celebrations and festivals are so very special, we wanted to share with you some favorite songs from these occasions. They are grouped together in the back of the book under the title song, "This Is the Day," which in itself is a song for a special day.

Three of our college-age girls have done the illustrations, thinking especially of what children would like (notice the shepherds and wise men portrayed as children in the Christmas section). It is our hope that the pictures and songs will make a book which will be most useful and most enjoyable to you, and that whoever you are—parent, teacher, grandparent, or lover-of-children—you will join voices with the children and "Sing through the Day."

Marlys Swinger

Contents

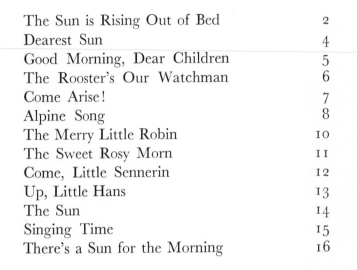

GOD MADE THE SHY, THE WILD ONES

DANCE TO THE MERRY PIPER'S SOUND

PIT, PAT, PAT

GOOD EVENING

THIS IS THE DAY!

The sun
is rising
out of bed

The Sun Is Rising Out of Bed

John Ferguson

English Folk Tune

Fast and lively

1. The sun is ris - ing out of bed, And in the East the sky is red; Then
2. The light is clear on hill and lea, The birds are loud in ev - 'ry tree; Then

up and wake each sleep - y - head, So ear - ly in the morn - ing. 'Tis
haste and rise and come with me, So ear - ly in the morn - ing. With

shame to dream the hours a - way, When all the world is bright with day, And
pleas - ant sights and sounds to spare, With hearts a - lert and free from care, We'll

Na - ture calls to work or play, So ear - ly in the morn - ing.
out and drink the whole - some air, So ear - ly in the morn - ing.

3. Where 'neath the share the furrows gleam,
We'll see the ploughman drive his team,
Or wander down beside the stream,
So early in the morning.
And where the water's fresh and cool,
We'll watch the trout within the pool;
There's time before we go to school,
So early in the morning.

Dearest Sun

Maisie Radford (English translation from Swedish)   Alice Tegner

Cheerfully

Dear-est sun, if you warm us Neith-er cold nor frost can harm us. Shine on
Dear-est sun, come and cheer us And the grass and bush-es near us. Let us

fa-ther and mo-ther and my great big bro-ther And my sis-ter tall,____ Shine
see you shine o-ver sheep and kine, O-ver horse and mill, O-ver

on us all. Shine the whole day-time through And please come back to-mor-row too!
vale and hill, O-ver land, o-ver sea And where-so-ev-er we may be!

4

Good Morning, Dear Children

Walter Rein

3 Part Round

Good morn-ing! Good morn-ing! Good morn-ing, dear chil-dren. Come out-side now, it is

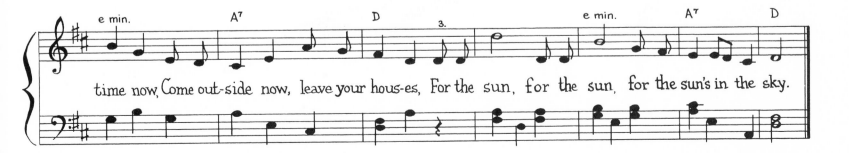

time now, Come out-side now, leave your hous-es, For the sun, for the sun, for the sun's in the sky.

The Rooster's
Our Watchman

Thuringian Folk Song

Merrily

1. The roos-ter's our watch-man, The lord of the farm is he, The lord of the
2. His crest is so hand-some, He looks like a king so grand, He looks like a

6

farm. / king. He wakes us both sum-mer and win-ter so ear-ly With crow-ing so lus-ty, with

*ki-ke-ri-ki-ki! Sing-ing tral-le-ra, **vi-de-ral-le-ra, Sing-ing tral-le-ra, vi-de-

ral-le-ra, With a***ruk-ke-tuk-ke and a ruk-ke-tuk-ke, Sing-ing ki-ke-ri-ki-ki!

3. With spurs on his two heels
   He's proud as a knight who rides,
   He's proud as a knight . . .

* pronounced: kee-kuh-ree-kee-kee
** vee-duh-ral-le-ra
*** rook-uh-took-uh

Come Arise!

2 Part Round

Johann Jacob Wachsmann

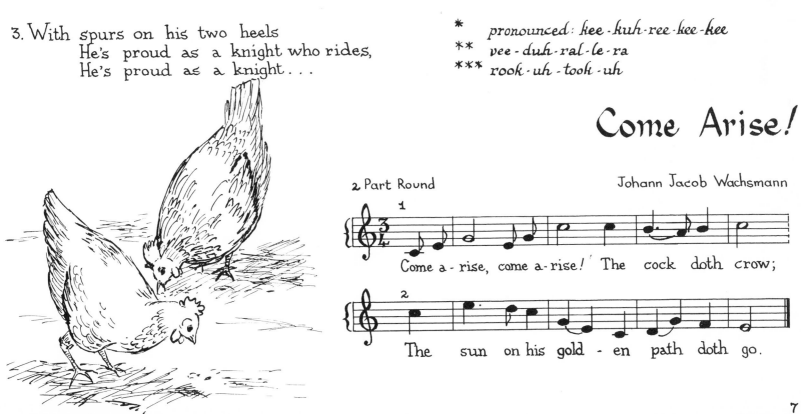

Come a-rise, come a-rise! The cock doth crow;

The sun on his gold-en path doth go.

7

Alpine Song

Swiss Folk Song

Very gay

1. Long be-fore the ris-ing sun Has his mer-ry work be-gun, Swift I climb the
2. Come my cows, come Spiess and Star, Young ones, old ones, near and far; Look, I have no

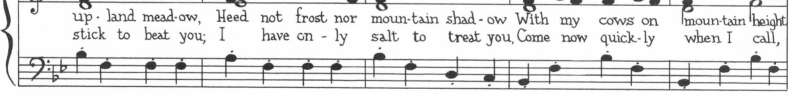

up-land mead-ow, Heed not frost nor moun-tain shad-ow With my cows on moun-tain height
stick to beat you; I have on-ly salt to treat you, Come now quick-ly when I call,

There is my de-light. _____
I have hay for all. _____ Ho-a, ho-a,*ho di-di, Ho di-ri di,

* ho-dee-dee, Ho-dee-ree-dee

8

Ho di-ri di, Ho-a, ho-a, ho di-di, Ho di-ri di, di-ri di.

3. Hear the milkmaids one and all
Singing as the echoes call.
They can milk and they can churn;
They can make the butter turn;
All their work is their delight
On the mountain height.

The Merry Little Robin

Nursery Song

Gently

There came to my win-dow one morn-ing in spring A sweet lit-tle rob-in, she came there to sing; The
Her wings she was spread-ing to soar far a-way, Then rest-ing a mom-ent seemed sweet-ly to say: "Oh

tune that she sang, it was pret-ti-er far Than an-y I heard on a flute or gui-tar.
hap-py, how hap-py the world seems to be, A-wake lit-tle girl, and be hap-py with me!"

The Sweet Rosy Morn

Richard Leveridge

Brisk and lively

The sweet ro-sy morn-ing peeps o - ver the hills, With blush-es a-dorn-ing the

mead-ows and fields;___ The mer-ry, mer-ry, mer-ry horn calls, Come, come, come, a-

way! A - wake from your slum - ber, and hail the new day.___ The day.___

Come, Little Sennerin

Swedish Folk Song

Come, lit-tle Sen-ne-rin, Call all the cows in, Put on your shoes, For it's
Hark, can you hear all the cow-bells a-ring-ing? Pull at the rope, Let the

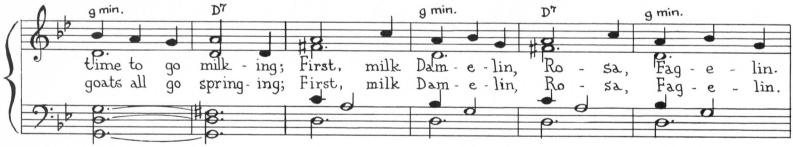

time to go milk-ing; First, milk Dam-e-lin, Ro-sa, Fag-e-lin.
goats all go spring-ing; First, milk Dam-e-lin, Ro-sa, Fag-e-lin.

Tu-tu-tu, the horn calls. Drive them home safe-ly when night falls.

Up, Little Hans!

Danish

Lively

D   G   D

1. "Up, lit-tle Hans! Up, lit-tle Hans! Hear the bird-ies sing-ing!"
2. "Up, lit-tle Hans! Up, lit-tle Hans! Soon will ring the school bell!"

A⁷   D

"No, Mom-my, No! No, Mom-my, No! Just the barn door swing-ing!"
"No, Mom-my, No! No, Mom-my, No! I don't feel at all well!"

3. "Up, little Hans!
Up, little Hans!
You may play your drum now!"
"Yes, Mommy, Yes!
Yes, Mommy, Yes!
Yes, I think I'll come now!"

13

The Sun

John Drinkwater

Marlys Swinger

Cheerily

I told the Sun that I was glad, I'm sure I don't know why; Some-how the pleas-ant

way he had Of shin-ing in the sky,____ Just put a no-tion in my head That

wouldn't it be fun___If, walk-ing on the

hill, I said "I'm hap-py" to the Sun.

*Instead of "I'm happy," children
may wish to sing "Good morning."

14

Singing Time

Rose Fyleman

Anonymous

Joyfully

I wake in the morn-ing ear - ly ___ and al - ways, the ver-y first thing, I

poke out my head and I sit up in bed and I sing and I sing and I sing and I sing and I

sing and I sing, _____ when I

wake in the morn-ing ear - ly. ___

There's a Sun for the Morning

Charles Ellerton
Thoughtfully

1. There's a sun for the morn-ing, And a moon for the night; When the
2. Light and warmth, joy and beau-ty Come from God high a-bove, And He

moon hides her face, Still the stars twin-kle bright.—When the bright.
gives these good gifts From a heart full of love.—And He love.

Attributed to W.A. Mozart

16

Come out

and play

Come Out and Play

Anonymous

Brightly

(summer) Come out and play!___ Bright is the day!___ Birds are all sing-ing, the
(winter) Come out and play!___ Bright is the day!___ Chick-a-dees sing-ing and

flow-ers are gay.___ Let's skip and run___ Out in the sun,___ Danc-ing and sing-ing, it
snow-men are gay!___ Let's skip and run___ Out in the sun,___ Slid-ing and skat-ing, it

is such fun. Jump-ing up, oh, so high!_Try-ing to reach the sky!_ Come out and
is such fun. Jump-ing up, oh, so high!_Try-ing to reach the sky!_ Come out and

play,___ Bright is the day;___ Birds are all sing-ing,_The flow-ers are gay.___
play,___ Bright is the day;___ Chick-a-dees sing-ing_And snow-men are gay.___

The Swing

Robert Louis Stevenson

Unknown

With a swinging motion

1. How do you like to go up in a swing,___ Up in the air so blue?___
2. Up in the air and o-ver the wall,___ Till I can see so wide,___

Oh, I do think it the pleas-ant-est thing___
Ri-vers and trees and cat-tle and all___

Ev-er a child can do!___
O-ver the coun-try-side.___

3. Till I look down on the garden green,
Down on the roof so brown —
Up in the air I go flying again,
Up in the air and down!

I Am Quite Big, But My Lisbeth Is Wee

Frances B. Wood

German Folk Tune

I am quite big, But my Lis - beth is wee,___ Lis - beth is
Dais - ies and but - ter - cups grow on the green,___ Grow on the

wee,___ For I am past five And my
green,___ With a gold and white crown I will

Lisbeth's just three.___
make Lis - beth queen.___

Let's Hike to the Woodlands Today

Thuringian Folk Song

Very jolly

1. Let's hike to the wood-lands to-day, Hal-lo, hal-li, hal-lo.___ The
2. We'll hunt where the mush-rooms all grow, Hal-lo, hal-li, hal-lo.___ And

ber-ries hang ripe on our way,___ Hal-lo, hal-li, hal-lo.___ Tra-la-la-la-
when we have picked them we'll go,___ Hal-lo, hal-li, hal-lo.___ Tra-la-la-la-

la, tra-la-la-la-la, Tra-la-la-la-la-la-la, tra-la-la-la.

3. We're jolly as elves in the wood,
Hal-lo, hal-li, hal-lo.
So merry our feast and so good!
Hal-lo, hal-li, hal-lo.

23

O Dandelion, Yellow as Gold

Noreen Bath

"O Dan-de-li-on, yel-low as gold, What do you do all day?"___ "I

just wait here in the tall, green grass Till the chil-dren come to play." "O Dan-de-li-on,

yel-low as gold, What do you do all night?"___ "I wait and wait till the cool dew falls And my

hair grows long and white." "And what do you do when your hair is white and the chil-dren come to

play?" "They take me up in their dim-pled hands, And blow my hair a-way."

Marie in the Meadow

Johann Trojan

Edwin Kunz

1. Ma - rie in the mead-ow, In the mead-ow Ma - rie, All the flow-ers and
2. Oh, I am so wor-ried, I've lost my Ma - rie; She's lost in the

grass-es are tal - ler than she.
clo - ver, Oh, where can she be?

3. But who is it sitting 'mid the flowers so bright,
   The harebells, the buttercups, the star daisies white?

4. This can't be a flower, a little head I see, —
   I've found her, I've found her, I've found my Marie!

25

The Bicycle

Jane Tyson Clement

Marlys Swinger

Off to an uneven start

It wob-bles and tips, I spill in a pud-dle. It flops on its side, Till I'm all in a mud-dle. It just won't go straight, the ped-als aren't there where I want them to be, But most an-y-where.

very smoothly

Then all of a sud-den with-out an-y warn-ing, I

cresc.

know how to ride,___ I know how to ride!___What a glo-ri-ous, glo-ri-ous morn-ing!___

The Magic Pony

Robert A. Coan

G. Meyerbeer

Quickly

Come and take a ride with me up-on my mag-ic po-ny!
Up and down the world we'll ride with not a thought of dan-ger,

Fast and far we'll trav-el, all the live-long day; He can car-ry
Swif-ter than the bree-zes, blow-ing wild and free; We will see the

two of us, for he is ve-ry strong, So you may come a-long, when I
strang-est sights in Eng-land, France and Spain, And then come home a-gain, when it's

ride a-way! So you may come a-long, when I ride a-way!____
time for tea! And then come home a-gain, when it's time for tea!____

The Fairy Flute

Rose Fyleman

Wolfgang Löwenthal

Smoothly

1. My bro-ther has a lit-tle flute Of gold and i-vo-ry,___ He
2. He plays it ev-'ry morn-ing And ev-'ry af-ter-noon,___ And

found it on a sum-mer night With-in a hol-low tree.___
all the lit-tle sing-ing-birds Lis-ten to the tune.___

3. He plays it in the meadows,
And everywhere he walks
The flowers start a-nodding
And dancing on their stalks.

4. He plays it in the village
And all along the street
The people stop to listen,
The music is so sweet.

5. And none but he can play it
And none can understand,
Because it is a fairy flute
And comes from Fairyland.

30

Dance, Little Maiden

(Translated from Swedish by) Maisie Radford

Alice Tegner

Lightly

Dance, lit-tle maid-en, Dance up-on the hill-tops, So do the fair-ies dance round the dew-drops!

Let all your steps be ve-ry, ve-ry light, For fair-ies would laugh at a hea-vy sprite!

God made the shy,

the wild ones

God Made the Shy, the Wild Ones

(Elizabeth's Carol)

Elizabeth Gould

Quietly, smoothly

H. S. Roberton

1. God made the shy,—— the wild ones Who live in field and wood;——
2. He taught them all —— the wis - dom And won - der of —— their ways.——

He taught them how—— to make their homes, And how to find their food.——
We love to learn a - bout—— them, And sing God's love and praise.——

I'm Little White Clover

Cicely Mary Barker

Olive Linnell

I'm lit-tle White Clo-ver, kind and clean, Look at my three-fold leaves of green;

Hark to the buz-zing of hun-gry bees, "Give us your hon-ey, Clo-ver, please!"

Yes, lit-tle bees, and wel-come too! My hon-ey is good and meant for you!

Bumblebees Are Humming

(Translated from Swedish by)
Maisie Radford

Alice Tegner

Bum - ble - bees are hum - ming: hum, hum. Pus - sies beat up - on the drum, drum.

Mice are danc - ing round the room, room. All the world is boom - ing: boom, boom!

The House of the Mouse

Lucy Sprague Mitchell

Marlys Swinger

The house of the mouse is a wee lit-tle house, a green lit-tle house in the grass, which

big clum-sy folk may hunt and may poke and still nev-er see as they pass____ this

sweet lit-tle, neat lit-tle, wee lit-tle, green lit-tle, cud-dle-down hide-a-way house in the grass.__

My New Pet Mouse

Jane Tyson Clement

Marlys Swinger

He wig-gled his whis-kers and looked up at me. Did he won-der if I was a queer kind of tree? He sniffed at my fin-gers and nib-bled my bread, Did he think that he was a-nib-bl-ing me, nib-bl-ing me in-stead? If I stay ve-ry qui-et and speak ve-ry low, Then may-be some morn-ing my mous-ie will know That I'm not good to eat, And I'm not a queer tree,— I'm me!

I Held a Lamb

Kim Worthington

Marlys Swinger

Gently

One day when I went vis-it-ing, A lit-tle lamb was there,__ I picked it up and

held it tight, It did-n't seem to care.__ Its wool was soft and felt so warm—like

sun-light on the sand,__ And when I gen-tly put it down It licked me on the hand.__

Dainty Little Butterfly

Wolrad Eigenbrodt

Edwin Kunz

Dain-ty lit-tle but-ter-fly, but-ter-fly, On the pur-ple heath-er;—
Dain-ty lit-tle flow-er blue, flow-er blue, Ring your bells so light-ly,—

Spread your lit-tle wings and fly in the sky, Wings as blue as heav-en.
That your but-ter-fly will hear and come near, Dain-ty lit-tle flow-er.

Worms

(for Jonny)

Gillian Barth

Marlys Swinger

Why does-n't Mom-my like worms in my pock-et? Not hair-y or scar-y, but squig-gly and
Mom-my says worms like a home in our gar-den—A-lone and un-known in a home 'neath a

wig - gly; I wish I could keep all my worms in my pock-et. But my

stone, so I think I'll put all of my worms in our gar-den.

Squirrel Nutkin

Frances B. Wood

Spanish Folk Tune

Lightly

1. Squir-rel Nut-kin has a coat of brown Quite the love-li-est in Wood-land Town.
2. Squir-rel Nut-kin in his coat of brown Scam-pers up the trees and down,
3. All the live - long__ day he plays In the leaf - y__ wood-land ways;

repeat for v.3 only

1. Two bright eyes look round to__ see__ Where the sweet - est__ nuts may be.__
2. Dash-ing here and swing - ing there, Leap - ing light - ly__ through the air.__
3. { But at night when squir - rels rest__ In a co - sy__ tree - top nest, }
   { Bush-y tail curled round his head, Mis - ter Squirrel goes off to bed. }

44

Song of the Bunnies

Margaret Wise Brown   Marlys Swinger

Bun - nies zip and bun - nies zoom __
Bun - nies jump and bun - nies run __

Bun - nies some - times sleep till noon __ Zoom Zoom Zoom Zoom __ All through the
Bun - nies al - so sit in the sun __ Run Run Run Run __ Run bun - nies

af - ter - noon __ Zoom Zoom Zoom Zoom __ This is the song of the bun - nies.
jump and run __ Run Run Run Run __ This is the song of the bun - nies.

45

The Obedient Kitten

French Folk Song

Lively

1. Oh, once there was a maid - en, Sing hey, hey, hey, and a roun-de-lay, Oh, once there was a
2. She made a cheese so tast - y, Sing hey, hey, hey, and a roun-de-lay, She made a cheese so

maid - en, Who watched her sheep all day, they say, Who watched her sheep all day.____
tast - y, One sun - ny sum-mer day, they say, One sun - ny sum-mer day.____

3. Her kitten sat and watched her,
Sing hey, hey, hey, and a roundelay,
Her kitten sat and watched her,
As any kitten may, they say,
As any kitten may.

4. "Now, kitty, keep your paws off!"
Sing hey, hey, hey, and a roundelay,
"Now, kitty, keep your paws off!
And see that you obey, I say!
And see that you obey!"

5. Oh, kitty kept her paws off,
Sing hey, hey, hey, and a roundelay,
Oh, kitty kept her paws off,
She found a better way, they say,
She found a better way!

47

Firefly

Elizabeth Madox Roberts   Croatian Air

Whimsically

{ A lit-tle light is go-ing by, A lit-tle light is go-ing by, Is go-ing up to
{ I nev-er could have thought of it, I nev-er could have thought of it, To have a lit-tle

see the sky, A lit-tle light with wings.
bug all lit,   And made to go   on   wings,   on wings.

Dance
to the
merry piper's
sound

Dance to the Merry Piper's Sound

Swedish Dance Song

Very Gay

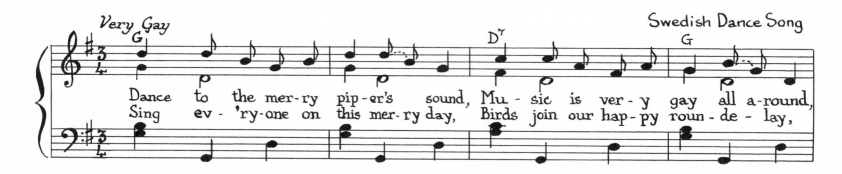

Dance to the mer-ry pip-er's sound, Mu-sic is ver-y gay all a-round,
Sing ev-'ry-one on this mer-ry day, Birds join our hap-py roun-de-lay,

Glad boys and girls are here to be found, While nim-ble feet are danc-ing.__
Fill-ing the air with mus-ic so gay, While nim-ble feet are danc-ing.__

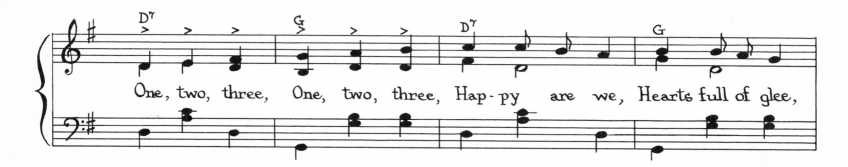

One, two, three, One, two, three, Hap-py are we, Hearts full of glee,

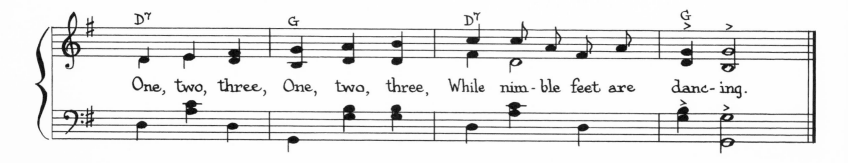

One, two, three, One, two, three, While nim-ble feet are danc-ing.

Oh, We Are Two Musicians

German

Oh, we are two mu-si-cians, We come from Mus-ic-land.__ Oh, we are two mu-

The circle dances left as Couple A, (hand in hand) goes around the inside to the right.

si-cians, We come from Mus-ic-land.__ We can play the vi-o, vi-o, vi-o-lin,

Everyone stops. Couple A face two more children (Couple B). All four imitate playing a violin, cello and a flute.

We can play the cel-lo and the flute.__ And we can dance and sing fa-la-la,__

Couples A and B skip around holding hands and all other children clap.

sing fa-la-la,__ sing fa-la-la,__And we can dance and sing fa-la-la,__ fa-la-la.__

For repeat of dance, Couple A returns to circle and couple B becomes the new couple A.

51

The Princess Was a Lovely Child

Old European Singing Game

1. The prin-cess was a love-ly child, love-ly child, love-ly child. The

The princess stands alone in center of circle of children.

prin-cess was a love-ly child, love-ly child. _____

2. She lived high in a castle tall,
   castle tall, . . .

   Children in the circle unclasp hands and raise them high over their heads.

3. There came a wicked fairy by,
   fairy by, . . .

   Children join hands. Child selected to be the wicked fairy goes around the outside of circle, then enters.

4. "Oh, princess, sleep one hundred years,
   hundred years, . . ."

   Wicked fairy sings and casts spell over the princess who falls asleep. Wicked fairy leaves.

5. A big, high hedge grew all around,
   all around, . . .

   Children in circle, keeping hands joined, raise arms high.

6. A gallant prince came riding by,
   riding by, . . .

   Child selected to be the prince rides around the outside of circle.

7. He chopped the trees down one by one,
   one by one, . . .

   Prince "chops down hedge" by breaking open the joined hands of the children.

8. "Oh, princess, wake and be my bride,
   be my bride, . . ."

   Prince enters circle and sings to the princess.

9. So everybody's happy now,
   happy now, . . .

   Prince and Princess dance together, and all the children skip in a circle clapping hands.

In and Out the Bonnie Bluebells

Old English Singing Game

In and out the bon-nie blue-bells, In and out the bon-nie blue-bells,

Children are in circle, holding joined hands high.
One child who is "It" weaves in and out of circle.

In and out the bon-nie blue-bells, For you are my part-ner.

"It" stops behind another child.

Pit-ta, pat-ta, pit-ta, pat-ta, On your shoul-der, Pit-ta, pat-ta, pit-ta, pat-ta, On your shoul-der,

With both hands "It" taps alternately
on the shoulders of child.

Pit-ta, pat-ta, pit-ta, pat-ta, On your shoul-der, For you are my part-ner.

On the repeat of the dance, the two children ("It" and partner with hands joined) weave in
and out of circle and stop behind two consecutive children. On the next repeat the four
54 children weave in and out. The dance continues till all children are following "It".

The Shepherd Maiden

French

I.

See a *Shep-herd Maid-en here Stand-ing with her sheep so near;___
With a part-ner she will make For the sheep a lit-tle gate.___

* or, "Shepherd Boy is here.."

II.

Run - ning quick - ly they will pass To the up - land mead-ow grass,___
* Shep - herd Maid - en, call them home; Day is done, no more they'll roam;___

* or, "Shepherd Boy now call them,.."

Where the past - ure is the best, Till the sun sets in the west.___
Safe with - in the guard-ed fold, Shelt-er them from harm and cold.___

(I) Shepherd Maiden (or Boy) stands alone in center of a circle of children. Repeat of (I): Shepherdess (or Shepherd) walks to one child at side of circle. Together they make a "gate" by clasping hands and raising them high.

(II): All the sheep go through their gate and "out to pasture". Repeat of (II): All the sheep go back through the gate and "home."

The Elfin Cap

German

Very jolly

A-round, a-round our cir-cle runs a point-ed Elf-in Cap, did-dle dum, A-round, a-round our

One child (the Elfin Cap) runs around inside of circle of children.
He puts his palms together over his head to make the "Elfin Cap."

56

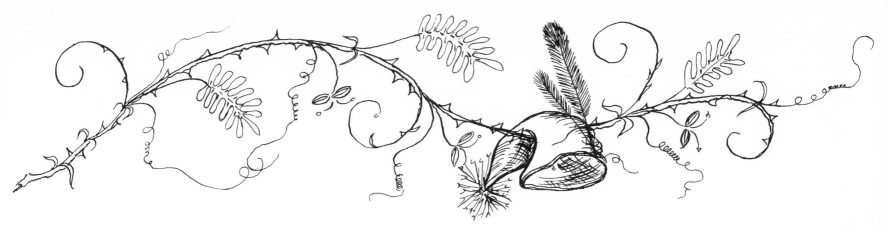

cir - cle runs a point-ed Elf-in Cap. Three times three is nine you know,

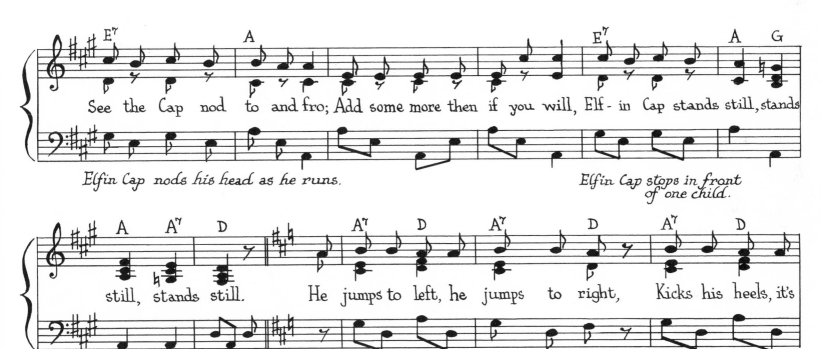

See the Cap nod to and fro; Add some more then if you will, Elf-in Cap stands still, stands

Elfin Cap nods his head as he runs.

*Elfin Cap stops in front
of one child.*

still, stands still. He jumps to left, he jumps to right, Kicks his heels, it's

Elfin Cap jumps left then right.

*He kicks heels behind
himself, standing in place.*

quite a sight, Then greets the new Elf Cap, Then greets the new Elf Cap.___

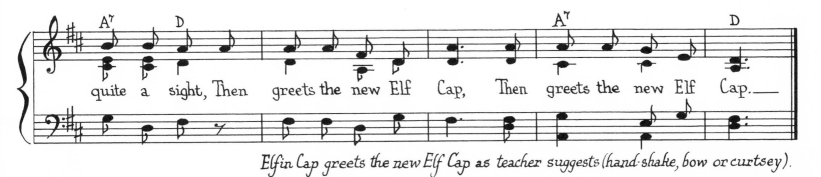

Elfin Cap greets the new Elf Cap as teacher suggests (hand-shake, bow or curtsey).

Cobblers' Dance

Danish

Merrily

F

Wind, wind, wind the bob-bin, Wind, wind, wind the bob-bin, Pull and pull and tap, tap, tap.

Children are in a circle facing center; they make winding motion with hands for one measure, reversing direction of the winding on the second measure.

Each child pulls elbows back two times.

Tap one fist on other fist three times

Skip-ping round and round we go, Light-ly, light-ly in a row.

Children skip around in a circle.

58

The Carpenters

South American

With vigor

1. The car-pen-ters are work-ing, Saw-ing the lumb-er. We love to watch them working, Saw-ing the lum-ber. They go *see*, we go *saw*, They go *see*, we go *saw*, Un-til we've sawed the lum-ber. Fin-ished at last!___
2. The car-pen-ters are work-ing, Pound-ing the nails in. We love to watch them working, Pound-ing the nails in. They go *bang*, we go *clang*, They go *bang*, we go *clang*, Un-til we've pound-ed the nails in. Fin-ished at last!___

Several "carpenters" are in center of circle. They make
motions and all the children imitate them.

3. Oh, see the masons working,
      mixing the mortar;
   We love to watch them working,
      mixing the mortar.
   They go *swish*, we go *swoosh*,
   They go *swish*, we go *swoosh*,
   Until we've mixed the mortar.
      Finished at last !

4. Oh, see the masons working,
      putting the bricks in;
   We love to watch them working,
      putting the bricks in;
   They go *clink*, we go *clank*,
   They go *clink*, we go *clank*,
   Until we've put the bricks in.
      Finished at last !

The Little Red Hen

Marlys Swinger

Lively

1. The Lit-tle Red Hen asked the La-zy Three, The Pig and the Dog and the Cat, "Who'll
2. The Lit-tle Red Hen asked the La-zy Three, The Pig and the Dog and the Cat, "Who'll

plant these grains of wheat for me?" "Not I," said each of the La-zy Three, The
cut this love-ly wheat for me?" "Not I," said each of the La-zy Three, The

Pig and the Dog and Cat.____ So the Lit-tle Red Hen with a chuck-le of glee plant-ed
Pig and the Dog and Cat.____ So the Lit-tle Red Hen with a chuck-le of glee cut

all the wheat with a fa - la - lee, Now what do you think of that ?____
all the wheat with a fa - la - lee, Now what do you think of that ?____

3...."Who'll take this wheat to the mill for me?"
...took the wheat to the mill with a fa-la-lee...

4...."Who'll make this flour into bread for me?"
...made the flour into bread with a fa-la-lee...

5. The Little Red Hen asked the Lazy Three,
The Pig and the Dog and the Cat,
"Who'll eat those loaves of bread with me?"
"I WILL," said each of the Lazy Three,
The Pig and the Dog and Cat.
But the Little Red Hen with a chuckle of glee
Ate all the bread with a fa-la-lee,
Now what do you think of that ?

Corn in the Wind

Rodney Bennett

Joan Bennett

Swayingly

Our hands are ears of corn,_____ Gold-en wav-ing corn,_____ And when winds

blow,_____ The oth-er way they go._____ *Wind speaks loudly:* "I am the West Wind." The west winds blow! "I am the East Wind." The east winds blow!

Whoo! Whoo! Whoo! Whoo!

O-ver to east we go._____
O-ver to west we go._____ That is the way the corn ears go When the Four Winds blow._____

One child takes the part of the wind. The others face north, raise hands above heads, constantly flutter their fingers and sing the first eight measures. (They are not sung again.) Children drop hands while Wind runs up on the west side and speaks, "I am the West Wind."

Children sing the rest of the song, bending over to the east on the first count of each measure as the Wind says, "Whoo!"
Repeat, with Wind running around to the other side and becoming the East Wind, then the South, then the North Wind. (Or a different child could be each different Wind)

64

Pit, Pat, Pat

Translated from Swedish by
Maisie Radford

Alice Tegner

Pit, pat, pat, go the lit-tle wet feet, Pit, pat, pat, pit, pat, pat. To be
boots soon dry when the sun comes out, Sun comes out, sun comes out;

out in the rain, what a treat, treat, treat. Pit,___ pat,___ pat.___ For the
Mo-ther is wait-ing and hears us shout, Hears__ us___ shout.__ When we

wet, for the wet does the chil-dren good, Chil-dren good, chil-dren good, When they
come in at last from our long, long day, Long, long day, long, long day, We get

sing as they walk as all chil-dren should, Chil-dren should. Our
brown bread and but-ter and curds and whey, Curds and whey.

1.
2.

Who Loves the Wind on a Stormy Night

Mysteriously

Anonymous

1. Who loves the wind on a storm-y night, When cur-tains are drawn and

fires are bright? He roars down the chim-ney, the win-dows he shakes, And all round the house such an up-roar he makes,____ Ooh____

Ooh____ Ooh____ says the wind.

2. He rocks the nests in the tree-tops high
And blows the kites right up in the sky;
He fills the sails of the ships so fine
And dries the washing hung out on the line.
  Ooh __, Ooh __, Ooh __, says the wind.

3. When snowdrops make their bravest show
And cold March winds begin to blow,
We know that in spite of the wind and the rain
That summer will soon be here again.
  Ooh __, Ooh __, Ooh __, says the wind.

Rain in the Night

Amelia Josephine Burr

Marlys Swinger

Lightly

Hear it rain-ing, rain-ing, rain-ing, Hear it rain-ing all night long; It is
There'll be ri-vers in the gut-ters And lakes a-long the street. It will

First time - Staccato;
Second time - Legato

some-times loud and some-times soft, And some-times like a song._____
make our la-zy kit-ty Wash his lit-tle dir-ty feet._____

The ro-ses will wear dia-monds Like kings and queens at court;_____ But the

pan-sies all get mud-dy Be-cause they are so short. I will sail my boat to-

70

mor-row__ In won-der-ful new plac - es, But first I'll take my wat-'ring pot And

wash the pan - sies' fa - ces,__ And wash the pan - sies' fa - ces.

71

Hi, Thunder!

Words and music by
the children of the
Macedonia Community

72

Mud!

Polly Chase Boyden

Marlys Swinger

Mud is ve-ry nice to feel All squish-y-squash be-tween the toes! I'd

rath-er wade in wig-gly mud Than smell a yel-low rose.___ No-

bod-y else but the rose-bush knows How nice mud feels be-tween the toes.

Boats Sail on the Rivers

Christina Rosetti

Marlys Swinger

Smoothly

Boats sail on the ri - vers, And ships sail on the seas;___ But clouds that sail a-

cross the sky Are pret-ti - er far than these.___ There are brid-ges on the ri - vers, As

cresc.

pret-ty as you please; But the bow that brid - ges heav-en, And o - ver-tops the

trees, And builds a road from earth to sky, Is pret-ti - er far than these.___

Oro, My Little Boat

Irish Folk Song

Flowing

1. O '-ro, my lit-tle boat that rests in the bay, O - ro ma var-din,
2. Sail-ing the waves o-ver foam-white crests, O - ro ma var-din,
3. Rid-ing the waves on the o-cean's rim, O - ro ma var-din,

Take up the oars and let us a-way, O - ro ma var-din.
Hap-py and free a-way to the west, O - ro ma var-din.
Sail-ing home as the light grows dim, O - ro ma var-din.

O - ro ma *cur-ra-agh O, O - ro ma var-din,

O - ro ma cur-ra-agh O, O - ro ma var-din.

*pronounced: Koor-ra-kee no

76

Sunshine and Rain

Words from Lithuanian Folk Song

Margarete Derlien

1. Sun-shine and rain, yes, both these must be,___ If from the seed shall grow forth a tree,___ But for my dar-ling two suns are nigh,___ So hush thy weep-ing, hush lul-la-by.___

2. Eyes of thy mo-ther keep thee in sight,___ Eyes dear and lov-ing, suns of the night,___ Ev-en to pure hearts comes once a sigh,___ So hush thy weep-ing, hush lul-la-by.___ Hush, lul-la-by,___ Blow wind so light,___ Hush, lul-la-by,___ Sleep now, good-night.___

3. Stars now are peep-ing, crad-led in peace___ Rocked in-to dream-land all cares shall cease,___ Sor-rows and troub-les they will pass by,___ Soon a new day dawns, hush lul-la-by.___

White Sheep

Unknown

Marlys Swinger

White sheep, white sheep, on a blue hill, When the wind stops You all stand still.

When the wind blows You walk a - way slow,— White sheep, white sheep, Where do you go?

The Earth Needs the Raindrops

J. Kartsch   A. Wagner

Slowly

The earth needs the rain - drops,
The tree needs a lit - tle branch

The day needs a light,
Where the bird builds his nest,

And heav - en needs lit - tle stars
And we need a lit - tle heart

When the day turns to night.
To love and to trust.

Good evening,
shining silver moon

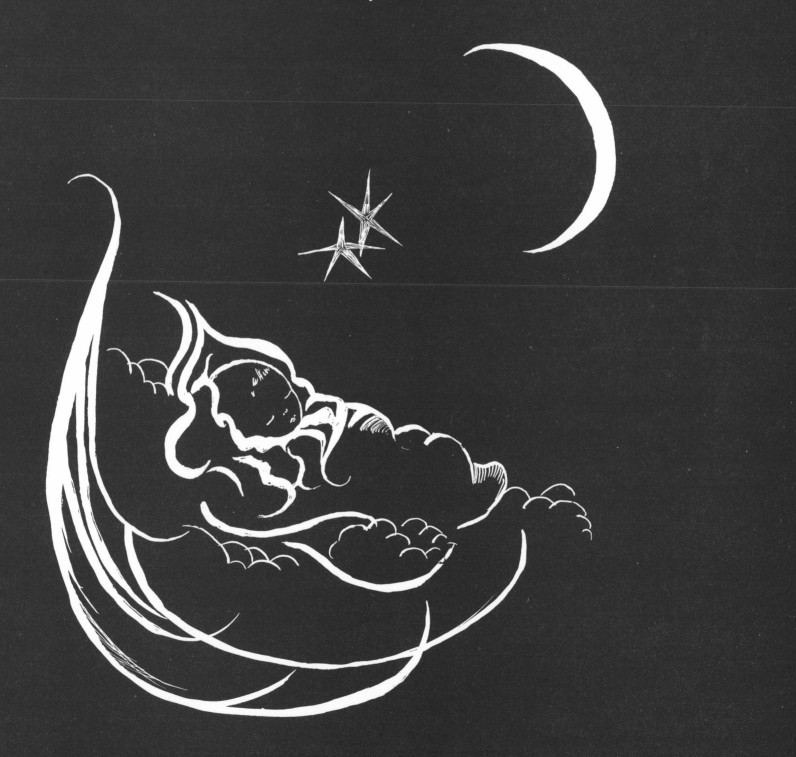

Good Evening, Shining Silver Moon

German Folk Song

1. Good eve - ning, shin - ing sil - ver moon! Where sail you there so high?___
2. My beams shall play a - round the beds Where hap - py chil - dren sleep;___
3. A - cross the wand'- rer's lone - ly path I'll send my cheer - ing ray;___
4. I sail, dear child, a - cross the sky That I each night may show___

I go to shine where field and wood In dark - ness lie!_____
Where birds are hid in down - y nest, My watch I'll keep._____
I'll twin - kle where the mer - ry elves And fair - ies play._____
The Great Cre - a - tor's ten - der love For all be - low!_____

Little Brother in the Cradle

Words and Music by a seven-year old boy for his new baby brother.

Very gently

Lit-tle bro-ther in the cra-dle, Now lie still and quiet, my ba-by, A little song I now am sing-ing, So that you will soon be sleep-ing. And then the an-gels come so quiet-ly And fly a-round your bed so light-ly, They kiss your lit-tle hand so soft-ly and cool your lit-tle cheeks so gent-ly, And love you ve-ry, ve--ry much.

Indian Lullaby

Henry W. Longfellow

Walter H. Aiken

Dreamily

1. Rock-a-bye, my lit-tle ow-let, In thy mos-sy, sway-ing nest,
2. Hush-a-bye, my lit-tle ow-let, Ma-ny voic-es sing to thee,

With thy lit-tle wood-land broth-ers, Close thine eyes and take thy rest. To whoo,___ to whoo,___ to
"Hush-a-bye," the wat-er whis-pers, "Hush!" re-plies the tall pine tree. To whoo,___ to whoo,___ to

whoo,___ to whoo.___
whoo,___ to whoo.___

3. Sleep, O Sleep, my little owlet,
Through our tent the moon shines bright,
Like a great eye it will watch thee,
Sleep till comes the morning light.
To whoo, to whoo,
To whoo, to whoo.

84

Little Red Bird

Manx Lullaby

Tenderly

Lit-tle red bird of the lone-ly moor, Lone-ly moor, lone-ly moor;

Lit-tle red bird of the lone-ly moor, O where did you sleep in the night?____

1. Out on a gorse-bush dark and wide, Dark and wide, dark and wide,
2. Did I not sleep on a sway-ing briar, A sway-ing briar, a sway-ing briar?
3. Wrapp'd in two leaves I lay at ease, Lay at ease, lay at ease, As

Swift rain was fal-ling on ev-'ry side, O hard was my sleep last night.____
Toss-ing a-bout as the wind rose higher, O lit-tle I slept last night.____
sleeps the young babe on its mo-ther's knees, O sweet was my sleep last night.____

Sleep, My Duckling

Finnish Folk Song

Gently rocking

1. Sleep, my duck-ling in the rush-es While the winds are blow-ing.
2. Sleep, my duck-ling in the rush-es, Night winds rock you gent-ly.

1. Where is your fa-ther, where is your mo-ther To sing you in-to slum-ber?
2. Sun-shine will warm you, waves will cool you, God will care for and love you.

87

Heidschi Bumbeidschi

Old Bavarian Folk Song

1. *A-ber heid-schi bum beid-schi, small bro-ther___ Sleep soft-ly the hours while thy mo-ther___ Is
2. A-ber heid-schi bum beid-schi, sleep sweet-ly,___ The an-gels are com-ing to greet thee;___They'll

*Pronounced: Ah-ber highchee boom by chee.

leav-ing her dar-ling for an-gels to keep___ And watch o'er her ba-by in dream-land a-sleep. Ab-er
wel-come you there for a ride in the sky___ A-cross the deep blue on a pon-y to fly. Ab-er

heid-schi bum-beid-schi, bum bum, (bum bum) A-ber heid-schi bum-beid-schi bum bum.___
heid-schi bum-beid-schi, bum bum, (bum bum) A-ber heid-schi bum-beid-schi bum bum.___

3. Aber heidschi bumbeidschi, in heaven
A pony snow white you'll be given,
And on it an angel
    with lantern so bright,
The loveliest star
    in the darkness of night.
Aber heidschi bumbeidschi bum bum,
Aber heidschi bumbeidschi bum bum.

4. The heidschi bumbeidschi comes riding,
My little one into sleep guiding,
He's taking him up
    to the star-dotted sky,
Good-night now, my baby,
    and sweet lullaby.
Aber heidschi bumbeidschi bum bum,
Aber heidschi bumbeidschi bum bum.

My Lantern

German

My lan-tern, my lan-tern, Sun and moon and star - light,
My lan-tern, my lan-tern, Sun and moon and star-light,

In the darkened heav-en high Shines no star with-in the sky.
Friend-ly lit-tle lan-tern bright, Be my sun and shield this night.

Dark-ened is the path this night With no moon or star as light.
Be my moon and star so high When no light is in the sky.

I Walk with My Little Lantern

Lively, gay

German

I walk with my lit-tle lan-tern, My lan-tern, my-self and I.___ Up
We walk with our lit-tle lan-terns, Our lan-terns so shin-y bright.___ We

yon-der bright lit-tle stars shine;___ Down here we're stars to the sky.___ The
wan-der through the dark-ness___ With wink-ing, twink-ling light.___ Like

new moon shines,_ The cat me-ows. *Eh!___ Eh!___ Eh!___ **La-bum-mel, la bum-mel, la
stars that swing_ Are lan-terns we bring.

*Rhymes with 'bay'　　　**La boom-a-la boom-a-la bay

beh!___ Eh!_ Eh!_ Eh!___ La bum-mel, la bum-mel, la beh!___

These two songs are from Germany where the children have the
lovely custom of walking and singing at night with lighted lanterns.

91

Wynken, Blynken, and Nod

Eugene Field

R. Houston Macdonald

With a gentle motion

1. Wyn - ken, Blyn - ken, and Nod one night___ Sailed off in the wood - en shoe,___
2. old moon laugh'd and sang a song, As they rocked in the wood - en shoe,___ And the
3. All night long their nets they threw To the stars in the twink - ling foam,___ Then
4. Wyn - ken and Blyn - ken are two lit - tle eyes,___ And Nod is a lit - tle head,___ And the

Sailed on a ri - ver of crys - tal light,___ In - to a sea of dew;___
wind that sped them all night long,___ Ruf - fled the waves of dew;___ The
down from the stars came the wood - en shoe,___ Bring - ing the fish - er - men home;___ 'Twas
wood - en shoe that sailed the skies ___ Is a wee one's trun - dle bed;___ So

Come to the Window

Unknown

(for Joseph)

Marlys Swinger

Moving gently

Come to the win-dow, my ba-by, with me___ And look at the

stars that shine out on the sea.___ There are two lit-tle stars that play games of Bo-

Peep___ With two lit-tle fish-es far down in the deep,___ And two lit-tle

frog-gies cry "Neap, neap, neap, neap,___ I see a dear ba-by that should be a-sleep."___

Which Is the Way the Wind Blows?

Dreamily

Old Dutch Cradle Song

1. Which is the way the wind blows__ Ov-er the sil - ver sea?__
2. Which is the way the wind blows__ Ov-er the sil - ver sea?__
3. Which is the way the wind blows__ Ov-er the sil - ver sea?__

Bring-ing a ship for fa - ther And a gold - en dream for me.__
Bring-ing a gown for mo - ther And a sil - ver shoe for me.__
Bring-ing a moon for mo - ther And a ti - ny star for me.__

Far in the Wood

Anonymous

Flowing

Far in the wood you'll find a well With water deep and
And all a-round the lit-tle well Are se-ven love-ly

blue; _____ Who-ev-er drinks by moon-light clear, Ti-ri ti-ra ti-
trees, _____ They rock and sway and sing a song, Ti-ri ti-ra ti-

ra-la-la-la, Will live a thou-sand years, _____ Will live a thous-and years.
ra-la-la-la, And whis-per in the breeze, _____ And whis-per in the breeze.

And through the seven lovely trees
The evening wind will blow,
And down fall seven little dreams,
Ti-ri. ti-ra. ti-ra-la-la-la,
My baby, all for you,
My baby, all for you.

Little Lambkin Sweet

Jane Tyson Clement   (for Abigail)   Marlys Swinger

Tenderly

1. Now the dark - ness creeps and my lamb - kin sleeps.___ Small stars
2. Day will come a - gain bring - ing sun or rain,___ Dais - ies
3. Now the dark - ness creeps and my lamb - kin sleeps___ Safe - ly

far a - way flick - er on and play___ Heav - en's games all night___ while your
at your feet, friend - ly dogs to meet,___ Balls to roll a - way,___ danc - ing
tucked a - way for a - noth - er day.___ May God's bless - ing rest___ by your

eyes shut tight,___ Lit - tle lamb - kin sweet, Lit - tle lamb - kin sweet.___
games to play,___ Lit - tle lamb - kin sweet, Lit - tle lamb - kin sweet.___
co - sy nest, Lit - tle lamb - kin sweet, Lit - tle lamb - kin sweet.___

Daisies

Frank Dempster Sherman   Winifred Dyroff

1. At eve-ning when I go to bed, I see the stars shine o-ver-head;
2. And of-ten while I'm dream-ing so, A-cross the sky the Moon will go,
3. For when at morn-ing I a-rise, There's not a star left in the skies;

They are the lit-tle dais-ies white That dot the mead-ow of the night.
It is a la-dy, sweet and fair, Who comes to gath-er dais-ies there.
She's picked them all and dropped them down In-to the mead-ows of the town.

Go to Sleep

American Folk Song

Rockingly

Go to sleep, go to sleep, ___ Go to sleep, lit-tle ba-by, ___ When you wake you shall

have ___ A coach and six lit-tle hor-ses, ___ Five lit-tle mice and three lit-tle rats, ___ A

coach and six lit-tle hor-ses, ___ Four lit-tle dogs ___ and two lit-tle cats, ___ A coach and six lit-tle

hors-es. ___ Go to sleep, go to sleep, ___ Go to sleep lit-tle ba-by. ___

100

Little Donkey Close Your Eyes

Margaret Wise Brown

Marlys Swinger

1. Lit-tle don-key on the hill Stand-ing there so ve-ry still Mak-ing fa-ces
2. Wild young birds that sweet-ly sing Curve your heads be-neath your wing; Dark night co-vers
3. Old black cat down in the barn Keep-ing five small kit-tens warm. Let the wind blow
4. Lit-tle child all tucked in bed Look-ing such a sleep-y head, Stars are qui-et

at the skies, Lit-tle don-key close _____ your eyes.
all the skies, Wild young birds now close _____ your eyes.
in the skies, Dear old black cat close _____ your eyes.
in the skies, Lit-tle child now close _____ your eyes.

This is the Day!

This Is the Day!

Psalm 118.24

T. Janet Surdam

This is the day, this is the day! This is the day that the Lord hath made. Let us re-joice in it, Let us re-joice in it, Let us re-joice in it and be glad. This is the day, this is the day — This is the day that the Lord hath made; Let us re-joice in it and be glad!

We Bring You Flowers

Sylvia Beels

With joy

We bring you flow-ers for love and joy, O Birth - day Child, to - day;___ Through
We wish you the glow of the sun by day, The shine of the stars by night;___ On your

rain and shine___ an - oth - er year Has passed a - long the way.___
path the gleam of the moon's soft ray And the fire - flies' twink - ling light.___

Shine, shine, lit - tle can - dle flame, In feast - ing take your part;___ And

as you burn your-self a - way, O shine in - to my heart.___ heart.___

105

Seasons' Birthday Song

Jane Tyson Clement

Marlys Swinger

Au-tumn, win-ter, sum-mer, spring, Birth-days are a time to sing; What-ev-er the sea-son,

rain or shine, It's a ve-ry spe-cial time.

Sing only the season's verse which is suitable.

(Spring) Pick a vio-let small and
(Summer) Wan-der sum-mer's mead-ow
(Autumn) Now the au-tumn leaves spin
(Winter) Since you are a win-ter

fair in the spring to deck your hair;
free; Choose your blos-som then tell me!
down, Weave the gold ones for your crown,
child Catch a snow-flake blow-ing wild,

And we will all join

in to say "Have a birth-day glad and gay."

birth-day glad and gay."

Birthday Roundelay

Kenneth Greenyer

Our lit-tle (Pe - ter) is (six) to - day. So now we all come sing - ing,

And in our hap - py roun - de - lay True joy and glad - ness bring - ing,

And in our hap - py roun - de - lay True joy and glad - ness bring - ing.

Joyful Greetings

Kenneth Greenyer

Joy - ful, joy - ful, joy - ful greet - ings, We come to wish you ev - ery - thing Of

good the com - ing year may bring; Wel - come, wel - come, to the Birth - day Child.

107

Autumn is Here

Margery Brinkmann

Briskly

1. Au-tumn is here and the leaves are all chang-ing, Red and
2. Au-tumn is here and the strong winds are blow-ing, Tos-sing the

faster

yel-low and rus-set and brown.____ Plums and cher-ries,
tree-tops and chas-ing the clouds.____ Scamp and scur-ry,

slower

nuts and ber-ries, Ap-ples and pears. Au-tumn is here.
rush and hur-ry, Tum-ble and toss! Au-tumn is here.

3. Autumn is here
          and the woodfolk all gather
  Lots of nuts for the
          cold winter days.
  Squirrels scatter, rabbits patter,
          moles creep along.
  Autumn is here.

4. Autumn is here
          and the harvest is gathered,
  Oats for porridge
          and wheat for our bread.
  Thank you, God, for bread and cheese
          and butter and milk,
  Thanks for our food.

109

Indian Harvest

Ethel Crowninshield — Traditional American

Moth-er Earth, to you we're sing-ing, Lis-ten to our song!___
On the trail where we are go-ing, Ev-er will we sing!___

Thanks for gold-en har-vest bring-ing, Lis-ten as we sing to you!
When the win-ter comes with snow-ing, Still our hearts will sing to you!

Sing to you! Sing to you! Songs of rain and sun-shine!___
Sing to you! Sing to you! Songs of rain and sun-shine!___

For the Golden Corn

E. Gould

E. Smith

Thoughtfully

For the gol-den corn, for the ap-ples on the tree, For the gol-den but-ter and the

hon-ey for our tea; For fruits and nuts and ber-ries that grow be-side the way, For

birds and beasts and flow-ers___ We thank Thee ev-'ry day.___

Easter Greeting

Laura E. Richards

B. J. Hancock

Brightly

The lit-tle flowers peeped through the ground, At Eas-ter-time, at
The pure white li - ly raised its cup At Eas-ter-time, at
'Twas long and long and long a - go, At Eas-ter-time, at

Eas-ter-time, They raised their heads and looked a-round, At hap-py Eas-ter-
Eas-ter-time, The cro-cus to the sky looked up At hap-py Eas-ter-
Eas-ter-time, But still the pure white li - lies blow, At hap-py Eas-ter-

time. And ev-'ry lit - tle flow'r did say,
time. And ev-'ry lit - tle flow'r did say, } "All peo-ple bless this
time. And still each lit - tle flow'r doth say,

ho-ly day, For Christ is risen, the an-gels say, At hap-py Eas-ter-time."

113

Easter Bunny Song

Jolly

Adapted from
Old German Folk Song

First comes the Eas-ter Bun-ny Pa-pa; Then comes the Eas-ter
They have soft suits all fur-ry and brown, With fluf-fy bob-tails

Bun-ny Ma-ma, And close be-hind on tip-py toe, The ba-by bun-nies in a row, And
white and round; Their Eas-ter walk they take at will A-long the fence and down the hill, Their

close be-hind on tip-py toe, The ba-by bun-nies in a row.
Eas-ter walk they take at will, A-long the fence and down the hill.

(Repeat first verse)

114

The Easter Hare

Edwin Kunz

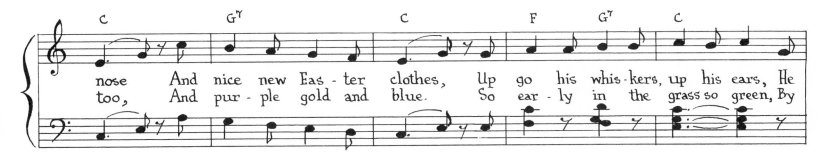

Very lively

Hel-lo, hel-lo, who's there? It is the Eas-ter Hare! With lit-tle twitch-ing
He makes an Eas-ter nest Of col-ored eggs the best, Of red and yel-low

nose And nice new Eas-ter clothes, Up go his whis-kers, up his ears, He
too, And pur-ple gold and blue. So ear-ly in the grass so green, By

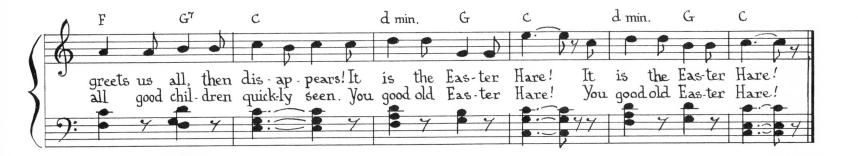

greets us all, then dis-ap-pears! It is the Eas-ter Hare! It is the Eas-ter Hare!
all good chil-dren quick-ly seen. You good old Eas-ter Hare! You good old Eas-ter Hare!

Heaven's Gate Has Opened

Shepherds' Christmas Song
Oberinn Valley, Austria

English by Inge Peinlich

Gaily

1. Now heav - en's gate has o - pened; we hear the joy - ous shout; See an - gel boys and
2. Now, friends, let's get to - geth - er to be the first of all To find and see the

116

an-gel girls a-rol-ling in and out! For ev-'ry boy and ev-'ry girl is
Ho-ly Child a-ly-ing in the stall: "Say, lit-tle boy, so gay and sweet, Do

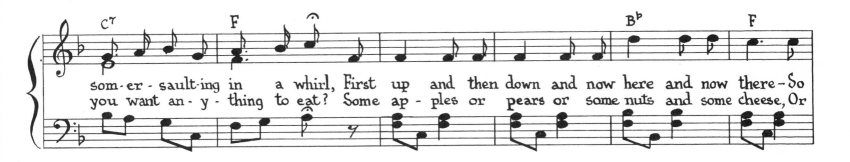

som-er-sault-ing in a whirl, First up and then down and now here and now there—So
you want an-y-thing to eat? Some ap-ples or pears or some nuts and some cheese, Or

grace-ful-ly and joy-ous-ly they're turn-ing ev-'ry-where. So where.
por-ridge full of nuts or an-y oth-er fruit you please? Or please?"

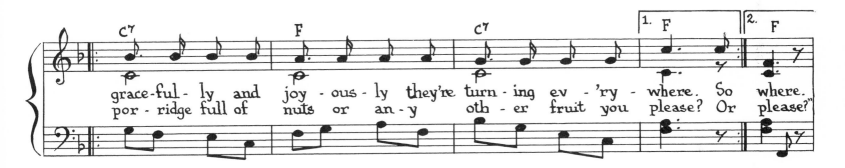

Hal-le-lu-jah, Hal-le-lu-jah, Hal-le-lu-jah, Ha-le-lu-jah.

Hallelujah!

Two-part round   Traditional

① Hal-le-lu-jah, Hal-le-lu-jah,

② A - men, A - men.

Go to Bethlehem

Traditional Czech

1. Come, and go to Beth - le - hem, Du-e dai, du-e dai, du-e dai, da;
2. Ja - cob, play your bag - pipe gai - ly, Du-e dai, du-e dai, du-e dai, da;
3. Mat - thew, play your flute so clear - ly, Du-e dai, du-e dai, du-e dai, da;

There we'll find Je - sus mild, In his cra - dle, lit - tle Child,
When we find Je - sus mild, In his cra - dle, lit - tle Child,
When we find Je - sus mild, In his cra - dle, lit - tle Child,

There we'll find Ma - ry mild, By his cra - dle, lit - tle Child.
When we find Ma - ry mild, By his cra - dle, lit - tle Child.
When we find Ma - ry mild, By his cra - dle, lit - tle Child.

Shepherds Come A-Running

Traditional Polish
Piano Acc. by Robert de Cormier

With gentle spirit

1. Shep-herds come a-run-ning in-to Beth-le-hem, Mer-ri-ly they sing and play their
2. Hap-pi-ly they of-fer him their gifts so sweet: Rai-sins, grapes and cit-rons, ap-ples
3. Mer-ri-ly the shep-herds all are danc-ing round. Shep-herds sing-ing, sheep bells ring-ing

pipes, hear them. Deep-ly now they bow to Ma-ry wond'ring how to greet the Child,
red for a treat. Rob-in of-fers him his spar-row, sing-ing soft-ly all the while,
pipes gai-ly sound! Deep-ly now they bow to Ma-ry, sing-ing fare-well to the Child,

Ti-ny Child: Deep-ly now they bow to Ma-ry, wond'ring how to greet the Child, Je-sus mild.
To the Child: Tom and Ni-co-de-mus bring a new-born lamb, a tink-ling bell; wish him well.
Ti-ny Child: Deep-ly now they bow to Ma-ry, sing-ing fare-well to the Child, Je-sus mild.

To Bethlehem I Would Go

Traditional Czech

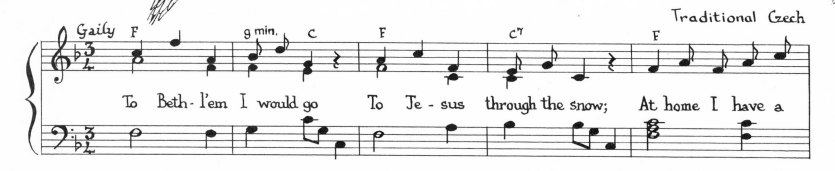

To Beth-l'em I would go To Je-sus through the snow; At home I have a

big, black cock so trim, A pret-ty cuck-oo that is brown and slim; These I will give to Him.

Black cock will make Him gay, Ne-ver will fly a-way: Pret-ty cuck-oo perch-ing near His head

Cal-ling sweet-ly to Him will make Him glad, Cu-cuck-oo, Cu-cuck-oo, Hail to Thee Ho-ly Je-su!

Birthday Presents

Paraphrase of the Japanese
Arranged from the Japanese

Lightly

1. Cup of warm milk, Ba - by Je - sus, Pre - sent from the Cow;
2. Wool-ly blan - ket, Ba - by Je - sus, Pre - sent from the Sheep;

She has given it for your birth-day. Drink it, drink it now!
It will be a soft white co - ver When you go to sleep.

3. If you're hungry, Baby Jesus,
   What will you eat then?
   Taste this brown egg, you will like it,
   Brought by Mother Hen.

4. Here's another present, Jesus,
   When you want some fun:
   On his back the donkey will take you,
   Riding in the sun.

Little Jesus Sleeps in the Hay

Very gently

Traditional Czech

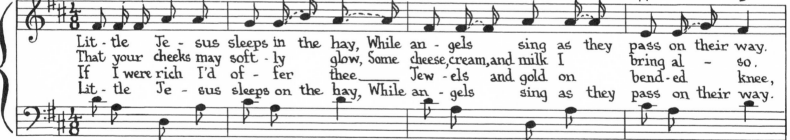

Lit - tle Je - sus sleeps in the hay, While an - gels sing as they pass on their way.
That your cheeks may soft - ly glow, Some cheese, cream, and milk I bring al - so.
If I were rich I'd of - fer thee____ Jew - els and gold on bend - ed knee,
Lit - tle Je - sus sleeps on the hay, While an - gels sing as they pass on their way.

Let us all now come near to sing, As gifts for the Child we bring.
Take them, sweet Je - sus, I pray! Long was my wear - y way.
But one thing I can sure - ly do — Play my sweet pipes for you.
We too will joy - ful - ly sing____ Praise to the new - born King.

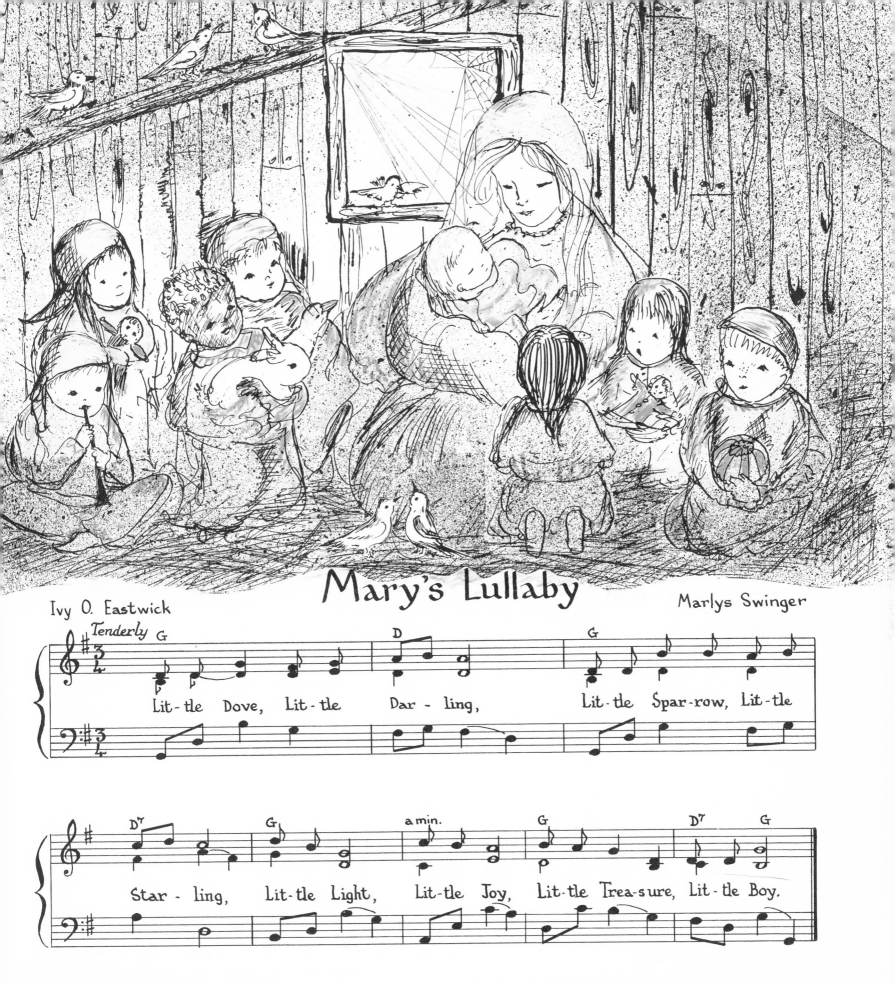

Mary's Lullaby

Ivy O. Eastwick

Marlys Swinger

Tenderly

Lit-tle Dove, Lit-tle Dar-ling, Lit-tle Spar-row, Lit-tle

Star-ling, Lit-tle Light, Lit-tle Joy, Lit-tle Trea-sure, Lit-tle Boy.

Agnes Leckie Mason

Three Kings

Phyllis Brown Ohanian

With a stately swing

1. Three kings trav-eled long from lands far a - way, Rid - ing by night and rest - ing by day.
2. They fol - lowed a star that shone ev-'ry night; Star that shone clear-ly, star that shone bright;
3. The kings gave Him gifts of in - cense and gold, Trea-sures they gave Him, treas-ures un - told.

Rid - ing on cam - els strong and tall, Rid - ing to see a Ba - by small.
Star that led them where Je - sus lay, Peace-ful - ly sleep - ing on the hay.
While the great kings bowed down their heads, Je - sus lay sleep - ing in His bed.

124

Hear All the Angels Singing

German

Joyfully

Hear all the an-gels sing-ing, Al-le-lu-ia!_____ Hear all the voic-es ring-ing, Al-le-lu-ia!

1. Glad choirs sing re-joic-ing, God's praise and glo-ry voic-ing. Al-le-lu-ia,__ Al-le-lu-ia.
2. The new-born King brings glad-ness To all who are in sad-ness. Al-le-lu-ia,__ Al-le-lu-ia.
3. To men on earth be giv-en True peace from high-est heav-en. Al-le-lu-ia,__ Al-le-lu-ia.

Index of first lines and titles

(*Titles that differ from first lines appear in italics*)

OTHER BOOKS
by THE PLOUGH PUBLISHING HOUSE

The Shepherd's Pipe: Songs from the Holy Night, a Christmas Cantata. The words by Georg Johannes Gick, set to music for children's voices or youth choir by Marlys Swinger. Beautifully illustrated in full-page color by Maria Arnold Maendel. All songs hand-lettered by Gill Barth.

The Rock and the Tower: The First Christians after the Death of the Apostles, by Eberhard Arnold. An unusual collection of early Christian sources covering the period A.D. 70-180. It will contain many texts so far inaccessible to the general reader, and gives comprehensive and challenging insight into the life and faith of the early Christians in a hostile, pagan environment.

Salt and Light: Talks and Writings on the Sermon on the Mount, by Eberhard Arnold. "This book has all the authentic ring of a truly Evangelical Christianity, and moves me deeply. It is the kind of book that stirs to repentance and to renewal." THOMAS MERTON

"*Salt and Light* is an admirable comment on the Sermon on the Mount. I wish the fullest measure of external and internal success to this excellent book so needed by today's world which turned against the Great Teaching of Jesus." PITIRIM A. SOROKIN

Behold That Star, a collection of fifteen outstanding Christmas stories from many lands including England, Spain, Holland, Germany, and the United States. Beautifully illustrated by Maria Arnold Maendel. Some of the authors include J. B. Phillips, Selma Lagerlöf, Jane Tyson Clement, and Elizabeth Goudge.

When the Time was Fulfilled: Talks and Writings on Advent and Christmas, by Eberhard and Emmy Arnold, Christoph Blumhardt and Alfred Delp. A companion volume to *Behold That Star*, as it expresses the deeper meaning of Christmas.

Love and Marriage in The Spirit: Talks and Writings, by Eberhard Arnold. In these talks and essays on the nature of man, and of woman, and on true marriage in the uniting power of God's love, Eberhard Arnold addressed himself to what he considered one of the main life problems of young people.

Children in Community, a photographic essay. This book is an intimate sharing of a precious part of our life in community, through full-page photos, short essays by Eberhard Arnold, other parents and teachers of the community, and by the children themselves.

Torches Together: The Beginning and Early Years of the Bruderhof Communities, by Emmy Arnold, telling of her memories which encompass the beginning, growth, setbacks, and struggles of the Bruderhof in Germany until the year 1937, when the Gestapo forced the group to leave Germany.

Eberhard Arnold. In this volume Emmy Arnold briefly recounts the life of her husband, Eberhard Arnold. Also included are recollections written by friends on the occasion of his seventieth birthday anniversary, and a selective bibliography of writings about and by Eberhard Arnold. This book is also available in German.

Inner Words for Every Day of the Year by Emmy Arnold. Each day brings you a "word" from the writings of men such as Eberhard Arnold, Christoph Blumhardt, and Dietrich Bonhoeffer, who tried to live out in daily practice their deepest faith regardless of the consequences.

Christoph Blumhardt and his Message, by R. Lejeune. Though virtually unknown to the English reading public, Christoph Blumhardt was one through whom many experienced the totally fresh and unconventional nature of Jesus' spirit.

The Sparrow, a collection of five stories and seven poems by Jane Tyson Clement. Beautifully illustrated by Kathy Mow. Jane Clement writes these stories out of a full heart and a sense of expectancy, a belief that something new for mankind is on the way. These stories are being published for the first time in this collection.

There are other books available from the Plough Publishing House, including some pamphlets and paperbacks. A complete, free catalog will be gladly sent on request.